IMAGES
of America

ANGWIN AND HOWELL MOUNTAIN

SIGN AT THE BASE OF HOWELL MOUNTAIN, 1962. This sign used to stand at the intersection of Sanitarium Road and Deer Park, right at the base of Howell Mountain. It greeted travelers leaving Napa Valley as they began their ascent toward the communities of Sanitarium (now Deer Park) and Angwin or points beyond. In this photograph by L.R. Callender, college students Marilyn Gordon and Lloyd Munson show off the newly placed sign. (Courtesy of Pacific Union College Archives and Special Collections.)

ON THE COVER: On the southern flank of Howell Mountain near Linda Falls, a rock outcropping juts over the valley. Known as Overhanging Rock, this destination commands views of Napa Valley from St. Helena to the bay. The rock is now on private property, but past generations of hikers knew and loved the vista point. In this photograph are four professors from Pacific Union College, possibly including Lydia and Guy Wolfkill on the left. (Courtesy of Pacific Union College Archives and Special Collections.)

IMAGES
of America

ANGWIN AND HOWELL MOUNTAIN

Katharine Van Arsdale

ARCADIA
PUBLISHING

Copyright © 2021 by Katharine Van Arsdale
ISBN 978-1-4671-0625-2

Published by Arcadia Publishing
Charleston, South Carolina

Printed in the United States of America

Library of Congress Control Number: 2020946892

For all general information, please contact Arcadia Publishing:
Telephone 843-853-2070
Fax 843-853-0044
E-mail sales@arcadiapublishing.com
For customer service and orders:
Toll-Free 1-888-313-2665

Visit us on the Internet at www.arcadiapublishing.com

*To my mother, Sharon Ann. Always a great reader and
my biggest fan, you would have loved this book.*

CONTENTS

Acknowledgments

I would like to thank those who helped me plan, research, and write this book, especially Nikelle Riggs at the Napa County Historical Society (NCHS), Peter Leuzinger and Jenifer Camarena of CalFire, Dewey Livingston at the Jack Mason Museum of West Marin History, my husband and proofreader William Bell, and my editor at Arcadia Publishing Caitrin Cunningham. I owe particular debts of gratitude to my intern Monica Heng and to my mentor Dr. Eric Anderson. Almost every photograph in this book comes from the Pacific Union College (PUC) Archives and Special Collections. Without the people of the past who saved these precious memories at PUC, there could be no book, and our lives would be much less rich today. Thank you.

INTRODUCTION

The world has heard of Napa Valley. Famous for sweeping vineyard views, lush gardens, and fine wines, the valley hosts almost four million visitors a year. But these are indeed visitors to the valley, and that is where their attention often lies. It is a rare thing to catch one looking up.

When they do look upward, the mountains greet them. Napa Valley is bracketed by the Mayacamas in the west and the Howells and Vacas in the east. Silverado Trail invites the visitor to wander up the valley ever northward, leaving Napa, Yountville, and Rutherford behind. If one travels along the eastern foothills, the trail will reach a crossing outside St. Helena. This is the road to Howell Mountain.

It is a curious name, Howell Mountain of the Howell Mountains. It earned this title from one of the first settlers on its slopes, John Howell. He once traveled with the Donner Party, before the snows fell, and came to California in 1846. A man of many talents, he built several cabins on the mountain. Out of one, Howell operated a blacksmith shop that served the residents of St. Helena. He must have been important, because somewhere along the way his name and the mountain came together, and it stuck.

If few people know about John Howell, it may be because for most historians of Napa Valley, Howell Mountain rarely merits a mention. This is surprising, and not just because of the eccentric man who gave the place its name. It is strange because the history of Howell Mountain is as old as Napa Valley and older even than the grapes.

John Howell built one of his cabins on a slope overlooking Glass Mountain and the future site of Elmshaven, a national historic landmark. However, long before any landmarks or Howell himself, Glass Mountain's rich obsidian deposits drew other people to this place. These were the Wappo, an indigenous tribe that populated Napa Valley before the Europeans came. One of their permanent villages, Tsemanoma, was just north and west of Howell Mountain, and the Wappo ranged from that settlement far and wide. From valley to summit, they left footpaths, grinding stones, arrowheads, and campsites on Howell Mountain and many other places now known by other names.

When explorers came to the valley, the first to settle down and stay was George C. Yount. He called Napa the paradise in which he wished to live and die. He made good on this wish by earning two Mexican land grants in his life. The first, Rancho Caymus, gave him a portion of the valley floor, where he would eventually found the town of Yountville. For the second, Rancho La Jota, he asked for Howell Mountain. The mountain proved to be a paradise too but perhaps one that drew the eye of a wilder bunch of pioneers who longed to live just a little closer to the sky.

Their names are half-remembered. Some we know, like John Morris, Edwin Angwin, Charles Krug, Adolphe Brun, and Jean Chaix. They found the mountain unforgettable. Its rich soil, plentiful springs, and unique Mediterranean climate provided the perfect environment for cultivation of every kind. Their plum trees, berry patches, pumpkins, and—yes—wine grapes grew in such abundance that some, like John Morris, became positively wealthy by selling the excess.

Warm days, cool nights, and clear air also attracted health seekers. Merritt Kellogg was one of the first to arrive when he established the Rural Health Retreat near Crystal Springs in 1878. Many others followed him. Soon, the mountain boasted half a dozen rustic resorts that offered an escape to nature for the Bay Area rich. One successful hotelier was Edwin Angwin, who opened his resort in the 1880s and gave the town of Angwin his name.

The beauty of Angwin's resort drew repeat visitors year after year. When the author Ambrose Bierce spent several months at Angwin's, he was entranced. "The weather up here is Paradisiacal," he wrote in 1893, on an afternoon in January, no less. In a March letter, he claimed "the fog is of superior opacity—quite peerless that way." By April, he was telling his friend, "We are blessed with the most amiable of all conceivable weathers up here, and the wild flowers are putting up their heads everywhere to look for you." Strolling across plowed fields and wading in the creeks, he often found arrowheads.

Another famous writer was likewise charmed by the location. Arna Bontemps, later a significant figure in the Harlem Renaissance, attended the college established at the site of Angwin's resort. When he graduated in 1923, he gifted his speech professor with a handwritten poem entitled "Dogwoods at the Spring (Howell Mountain)," in which he imagined himself as a prodigal son. "I shall return when dogwood flowers are going," he wrote, "knowing / The old unanswered question on your mouth." The frost would be "on the manzanita shoots" and "dogwoods at the spring" would be turning brown in his moment of autumnal reflection about mortality.

This school Bontemps attended, Pacific Union College, came to the mountain in 1909. It became the heart of the tiny town of Angwin, drawing some students for a season and others for a lifetime. The first graduate recalled her time there some 50 years later, saying "The sun did not always shine at Angwin. There are those who maintain nowadays that it never rains as it did then. But in between the burning sun and the pelting rain there were days so perfect that the Angwin-bred will be lonely for them wherever he goes." It seems she spoke from personal experience.

A theme develops across the history of Howell Mountain and the memories its inhabitants share. It is a distinctive place—higher, cooler, and wilder than its famous neighbor, Napa Valley. It deserves to be remembered in words and photographs. Indeed, although these photographs can never capture the crashing of Linda Falls or the smell of pine needles warmed by the sun across the forest floor, they ask the reader to imagine how Howell Mountain looked to those pioneers who chose to brave the steep and winding road to the summit. There were many of these mountaineers. The natural beauty of Howell Mountain has been the backdrop for intense human striving, from the hunter-gatherers of prehistoric times to the farmers, builders, educators, and other visionaries of the American era. Their successes have both enhanced and changed the natural beauty of the mountain. Through transition, growth, and even loss, Howell Mountain continues to cast its spell.

One

2000 BC TO 1822

Picture the early days of Napa Valley. Fog rolls up from the bay, blanketing the Mayacama Mountains in the west and the Howells and Vacas in the east. In the eastern ranges, one distinctive peak rises almost 2,000 feet. It is Howell Mountain. Here, the easternmost stands of coastal redwood grow alongside pine, fir, oak, and manzanita. Creeks tumble down waterfalls split by giant boulders, evidence of volcanic eruptions long ago. There are no roads, but there is a footpath that leads from the valley floor to an open plain near the summit. A spring-fed creek runs through a willow swale in the center of the plain. Near the water are large outcroppings of stone, pockmarked with dozens of mortar holes. These acorn grinding holes are the enduring evidence left by the Wappo people who call Howell Mountain home.

The Wappo are industrious people whose lives are defined by changing seasons and a wild environment. They share berry patches and fishing holes with grizzlies and manage their land by setting purposeful fires. They call the month of June "Burn-the-Valley Moon."

On Howell Mountain, in the heart of future Angwin, the Wappo camp in a small village of oval-domed huts with excavated interiors. Town children of the 1930s will play in one of these remaining circular depressions in the ground near Sky Oaks Drive. But for now, the Wappo live here, splitting their days between work in the forest and recreation in the dance pavilion or sweat lodge. Inevitably, white settlement will someday disrupt and destroy the Wappo and their way of life. However, with every rainstorm or plough furrow that turns up a long-lost spearpoint or arrowhead, the land itself will remind all newcomers that others once called this mountain home.

VIEW OF SENTINEL HILL. Howell Mountain is a peak about 1,700 feet in elevation in the eastern hills overlooking Napa Valley. The mountain drops off steeply toward Pope Valley to the north and east, Lake Hennessey to the south, and Napa Valley to the west. Deep canyons cut into the mountain slopes on all sides. Conn Creek, which travels through the Angwin plateau, plunges down Linda Falls and runs south to Lake Hennessey and the Conn Creek Dam. Because the land here is volcanic, some early settlers believed the plateau near the mountain summit was an extinct crater. It is not, but the hills are covered with red volcanic clay with scoria, and loose volcanic rock lies scattered in many places.

FOREST NATURE TRAIL. Some of the first people known to live on Howell Mountain were the Wappo Indians, part of the Yuki linguistic family. Their territory stretched from present-day Napa to Cobb Mountain in the north. Historians estimate that anywhere from 1,000 to 6,000 people may have lived in Napa Valley prior to European settlement. Primarily nomadic, the Wappo traveled from spring to fall, returning to small permanent villages each winter. One of these villages was on Howell Mountain.

HOWELL MOUNTAIN OAK TREE. Several natural features made the meadows and forests of Howell Mountain a compelling home for the Wappo. The presence of many vigorous natural springs kept water flowing through Conn Creek even at the height of summer. The water attracted game such as rabbits or deer, which the Wappo killed with obsidian-pointed arrows made with stone from the quarries at nearby Glass Mountain. But most importantly, the forests were rich with acorn-laden oaks.

WAPPO MORTAR AND PESTLE. The staple food of the Wappo was pinole, or acorn meal. Women performed the seasonal acorn harvest, but both men and women prepared the acorns through a laborious many-step process. First the acorns had to be leached of bitter tannins by several rinses in warm water. The Wappo then ground the acorns to a fine flour in stone depressions like this portable mortar or in a rocky outcrop near their dwellings. They cooked the flour into porridges or bread.

GRINDING TOOLS IN STONE TROUGH. The grinding tools pictured here all come from the collection of John Fisher, a longtime resident of Howell Mountain. Like many other examples held by private collectors, they were uncovered on his property during various construction or agricultural projects over the years. For as long as anyone can remember, Howell Mountain residents have easily discovered artifacts like these.

WAPPO BEADS FROM FUNERAL MOUND, 1972. Before the influence of Spanish missionaries, the Wappo cremated their dead. After 1823, however, they transitioned to burial in funeral mounds near permanent villages. The beads pictured here came from a grave near Napa, but Howell Mountain is a resting place for the Wappo as well. In the 1920s, locals often hiked to the "Indian Graveyard" to view over a dozen mounds. Funeral mounds were excavated in Las Posadas Forest around 1900. (Courtesy of the NCHS.)

WAPPO WOMAN. Although the Wappo were primarily patriarchal, women received respect in their society. Marriages were monogamous, and divorce was possible with mutual consent. Most work was divided along gender lines, but on rare occasions, women could ascend to tribal chief. When a woman gave birth, her husband practiced couvade, a ritual that confined him to bed alongside his wife for four days. (Courtesy of the NCHS.)

SPEAR POINT AND OBSIDIAN SHARDS. The bow and arrow was the Wappo's main weapon. Bows made of manzanita wood were paired with arrows tipped with obsidian points. The obsidian was mined at the base of Howell Mountain at the Glass Mountain quarries. The site at Glass Mountain provided the Wappo and surrounding native populations with an almost inexhaustible supply of obsidian for arrows, spears, knives, darts, and ceremonial blades. So many were manufactured that Angwin locals still find new arrowheads after a hard rain.

HOWELL MOUNTAIN VIEW THREE MILES FROM ANGWIN. When settlers reached Napa Valley, as many as 6,000 native people lived there. Unfortunately, arriving settlers heralded the end for the Wappo by way of violence and disease. The land, however, remained home. In the 1870s, Elvira Angwin unexpectedly met a Wappo man outside her cabin. He came to see his childhood home, he said, here on the mountaintop. After a moment of quiet reflection, "he went up and away over the hills," never to return.

Two

1823 to 1848

Life changed dramatically for Napa Valley in the summer of 1823. An adventurous young priest from Barcelona, Fr. José Altimira, traveled north out of San Francisco in search of a site to establish the last and northernmost Catholic mission. Altimira settled on Sonoma, but he set foot in Napa Valley that summer, making him the first recorded European to enter this fertile stretch of Alta California. In his diary, Altimira wrote that the soil was good for pasture, although littered with enough rocks to "build a new Rome."

When the Mexican government secularized the missions in 1833, Father Altimira's mission transferred from Catholic hands to the control of Gen. Mariano Guadalupe Vallejo. It was General Vallejo's former carpenter, George C. Yount, who became the first permanent resident of Napa Valley when he received the Rancho Caymus land grant. The pioneer era had fully begun.

Unlike the valley floor, Howell Mountain attracted settlers slowly. Yount, however, saw the great potential of the forests, and turned his attention to the mountain. Through careful campaigning, Yount received Howell Mountain in the Rancho La Jota land grant in 1843. This made him the proud owner of land where "some of the trees were six feet through at the base, straight as arrows, and 150 feet high," according to historian Walton Brown.

Wagon trains began to trickle over the Sierras, bringing workers to fell the forests. Clever Yount hired a father and son, Isaac and John Howell, to live at Rancho La Jota and deal with "grizzlies and natives." Yount promised them land in exchange for their services, but he never wrote the promise down. The Howells lost much of their squatters' claim in the end, as did many neighbors in similar straits, but they left their family name on the mountain they had tamed.

Gen. Mariano Guadalupe Vallejo. General Vallejo served Spanish, Mexican, and American governments during his time presiding over the land that would become Napa and Sonoma Counties. From the presidios of San Francisco and Sonoma, Vallejo oversaw the conquest of natives, the defeat of Russians from the north, and the colonization of the North Bay. The general's brother Salvador helped settle Napa Valley. Salvador received the Napa Rancho from Mexico in 1838 and established a ranch there. (Courtesy of the NCHS.)

GRAVE OF GEORGE C. YOUNT AND MAP OF LA JOTA RANCHO. The photograph at right shows the grave of George C. Yount, a pioneering trapper who arrived in Napa Valley in 1831. Yount worked briefly as a carpenter for General Vallejo. Through the support of the general, Yount received two land grants from Mexico. The first was Rancho Caymus in 1836, and the second was Rancho La Jota in 1843. The La Jota parcel encompassed one square league of land surrounding Howell Mountain. Yount never lived on his La Jota land, but he logged the forests. After his death, the land passed to his descendants and was split up and sold to many of the families whose names now appear on neighborhoods and road signs on the mountain.

Sawmill on Howell Mountain, 1900s. When George Yount received the Rancho La Jota land grant from Mexico in 1843, he specifically requested that the 4,000-acre stretch include heavily wooded Howell Mountain. Yount knew the value of the forest and its mix of oak and redwood. He intended to build a sawmill to fuel his business in Napa Valley. Although Yount never logged the mountain as extensively as he intended, those who followed him continued the industry. Edwin Angwin and others constructed mills along Conn Creek, near Linda Falls, and in present-day Mill Valley near Howell Mountain's summit.

LINDA FALLS. On Howell Mountain, water is plentiful even during times of drought thanks to countless freshwater springs. Springs feed Conn Creek, which is named for Conley Conn, who settled the area in the 1840s. Conn Creek tumbles down Linda Falls toward what is now Lake Hennessey. Linda Falls, pictured here, has drawn admirers from the Wappo people to pioneers to local hikers today.

PIONEER CEMETERY IN LAS POSADAS FOREST. Moore Creek cuts through Las Posadas Forest and flows down the eastern flank of Howell Mountain. This forest, which is now owned by the state, was home to several early pioneer families who left their mark. Very little is known about the Moores for whom the creek is named, except that Mr. Moore came from Ireland and settled on Howell Mountain in the early 1840s as a squatter. After his wife died under suspicious circumstances, Moore disappeared from his squatter's claim. In 1878, John Morris purchased the land, built a redwood cabin for his family, and began to ranch. While others planted wine grapes, Morris cut and sold redwood stakes to the vineyards. Seven members of the family, including John Morris and his mother, Sally, were buried in the rustic cemetery that lies in Las Posadas beyond the 4H camp.

PRUNE ORCHARD. The Morris family lived in relative poverty before purchasing Moore's squatter's claim. However, the temperate climate and long growing season on Howell Mountain quickly brought the Morris ranch financial success. Their crops of berries, apples, peaches, plums, and pears sold quickly in local markets and later supplied many health resort visitors with food. The prune orchard pictured here was planted by Edwin Angwin, their neighbor.

WINERY WORKERS EMPLOYED BY CHARLES KRUG. Howell Mountain's relationship with the wine industry begins with George Yount, who planted Napa Valley's first wine grapes in 1839. However, if Yount planted grapes on his La Jota Rancho grant, no records remain. A Prussian immigrant named Charles Krug was among the first grape growers on Howell Mountain, where he planted over a hundred acres of vines. Krug came to the United States in 1847 and established the first commercial winery in Napa Valley in 1861. (Courtesy of the NCHS.)

UNPAVED ROAD UP HOWELL MOUNTAIN. The Howell Mountain road has always been infamously steep and high. "Naturally, the Howell Mountain grade is a marvel in scenic beauty," the *St. Helena Star* reported on its front page, but summer dust and winter mud made travel extremely difficult. When Mrs. Moore of Las Posadas died suddenly, neighbors from miles around cooperated to carry her coffin down to the St. Helena Cemetery.

DEVIL'S PUNCHBOWL. On the northwest side of Angwin, Bell Creek flows past Rattlesnake Ridge and through the forest until it falls into a deep basin of water known as Devil's Punchbowl. It is not known what the Wappo called this waterfall before the Bell family claimed the land, but the Punchbowl has always been a beautiful destination and an important Howell Mountain water source.

VALLEY VIEW FROM HOWELL MOUNTAIN. As the 1840s drew to a close, the valleys around Howell Mountain began to change. Where once deer and grizzlies wandered floodplains crisscrossed by creeks on their way to the bay, there were now homesteads and the furrows of ploughs. This photograph, taken a few decades later, shows the changes the early Howell Mountain pioneers watched develop from their vantage point almost 2,000 feet above the valley floor.

Three

1849 TO 1908

The second half of the 19th century brought a series of booms to California, some of them quite particular to Napa Valley. The end of the Mexican-American War in 1848 plucked the land out of Mexico's hands just in time for the Gold Rush of 1849. Although the hills surrounding Napa Valley never earned a reputation for rich gold or silver mines, they attracted miners of chromium, mercury, magnesite, manganese, and asbestos, among other minerals.

While some men grubbed under the ground to make their fortune, others turned their eyes to the hills and valleys with a mind toward agriculture and viticulture. The pleasant Mediterranean climate of Napa Valley was perfectly suited to farming. A long growing season of warm, dry, sunny days followed by cool evenings and foggy mornings provided an ideal combination for fruit of all kinds and fine wine grapes in particular. In 1880, when Rancho La Jota was divided into lots and sold at auction, winemakers such as Charles Krug, John Thomann, and Adolphe Brun and Jean Chaix purchased parcels and planted grapes.

With the influx of agriculture came a network of new roads, all of them unpaved and incredibly dangerous. The Woodworth-Muller family transported their casks of wine down Howell Mountain only two barrels at a time due to the steep grade of the road. Barrels were offloaded beside the road and left unattended while the driver headed back to the ranch to get more. Local legend tells of an opportunistic neighbor who helped himself to several barrels before Frank Muller caught him in the act and fired a warning shot past his hat.

Despite the occasional Wild West–style altercation, the mountain attracted more settlers. Many came for the clear, dry air, which served as a remedy for tuberculosis, asthma, or general malaise. Entrepreneurs such as Edwin Angwin, Merritt Kellogg, Charles Henne, the Tolands, and the Woodworths opened health retreats and rustic resorts all over Howell Mountain. While most of these resorts enjoyed a heyday around the turn of the 20th century, the Rural Health Retreat changed with the times and became a hospital and nursing school. The first male nursing graduate in California earned his degree there on the slopes of Howell Mountain.

NEVADA COTTAGE BUILT BY JOHN HOWELL, 1860s. This cottage was probably built by John Howell, St. Helena's blacksmith. He sold the building to Edwin Angwin in 1874, and it passed to Pacific Union College in 1909. According to local legend, Howell Mountain is named for the Howell family who ranched near Angwin until 1868. The family, under the direction of father Isaac Howell, joined a wagon train west in 1846. At Fort Bridger in Wyoming, the Howells met the Donner Party. There the entire group was convinced to take a southern cutoff into California to avoid Indian trouble on the Oregon Trail. Luckily for the Howells, Isaac was accompanied by his adult children, including John Howell. With the help of his sons, Isaac Howell passed through the Sierras ahead of the Donner and Graves families. On October 27, the Howells were the last emigrants to pass Truckee Lake just days before snowfall began, infamously trapping the Donner Party for the winter. Both Isaac and John Howell joined rescue parties that attempted to reach the Donners in January 1847, but it was April before the last stranded members were saved.

MERCURY MINE NEAR HOWELL MOUNTAIN. In addition to ranching, early settlers near Howell Mountain often earned a living by mining mercury, chromium, or asbestos. This mine on the slopes of Mount St. Helena is a local example. Rather than mercury, mines on Howell Mountain were known for kalinite and volcanic rock. The high school in St. Helena was built in 1912 from Howell Mountain quarry rock.

ORE CART USED FOR EXCAVATION IN ANGWIN. Even when a local mine closed, the community still benefited from the industry. These ore carts and track were purchased from an old Aetna Springs mercury mine and used in the construction of Irwin Hall. Construction workers filled the carts with volcanic ash and dirt excavated from the hillside, which they dumped to create the promontory where Irwin Hall now stands.

WAGONS HAUL A GRAPE HARVEST ON HOWELL MOUNTAIN, 1900S. The history of wine grapes on Howell Mountain began with the family of George Yount, the Napa Valley pioneer who first planted grapes in the valley in 1839. During the 1870s, the husband of Yount's granddaughter, William Campbell Watson, purchased over half of Yount's old Mexican land grant and planted vineyards on the land. By 1880, according to the *St. Helena Star*, "The grape boom has reached Howell Mountain. Mr. Watson has already sold some twelve or thirteen hundred acres off the La Jota Rancho, of 100 acres to 160 acres each, for grape growing purposes. . . . Messrs. Charles Krug and John Thomann [of Sutter Home Winery] will commence operations soon." Even during the Phylloxera plague that struck in the 1890s and until Prohibition in 1919, mule-drawn wine wagons like these were a frequent sight on the winding mountain roads.

BURGESS CELLARS WINERY, BUILT AROUND 1882. One of the earliest wineries built on Howell Mountain is still in operation today. Burgess Cellars, previously known as Souverain Cellars, was built in the early 1880s along today's Deer Park Road. During Prohibition, the tanks of wine were sealed, and Peter Stark lived at the winery and ran a chicken ranch. However, after the Volstead Act's repeal, Burgess Cellars returned to business and became bonded winery No. 946.

HOWELL MOUNTAIN VINEYARDS, BUILT 1886. This three-story winery building on White Cottage Road was constructed in 1886. Italian craftsmen cut the block, while Chinese laborers assembled the building. Howell Mountain Vineyards joined neighboring wineries such as Hess and Liparita in growing vines imported from Medoc, France. Howell Mountain grape growers focused on zinfandel and cabernets, and their wines won awards in Paris in 1889 and 1900.

Main Entrance
St Helena Sanitarium
Sanitarium, California

RURAL HEALTH RETREAT, ESTABLISHED 1878. In 1871, William A. Pratt purchased a tract of land about three miles from St. Helena at Crystal Springs. At the time, he had no plans to establish a hospital of any kind, but in 1873, he met J.N. Loughborough, an Adventist minister. Noting the clean mountain air and spring water, Loughborough told Pratt that his location was perfect for a health resort. Just a few years later, a doctor of hydrotherapy named Merritt Kellogg offered to contribute $1,000 if Pratt would donate the land and join him in building a retreat dedicated to Adventist health principles. Pratt agreed. Along with A.B. Atwood of St. Helena, the men raised $5,000. Kellogg himself swung the pickaxe that broke ground on the Rural Health Retreat, which would become the St. Helena Sanitarium and later St. Helena Hospital.

MAIN BUILDING

MERRITT G. KELLOGG, AROUND 1900. Merritt Gardner Kellogg founded the St. Helena Sanitarium and was the first Seventh-day Adventist to settle in California. Kellogg came from a health-conscious family. His stepbrother, W.K. Kellogg, invented corn flakes. Another brother, John Harvey Kellogg, served that cereal to patients at the Battle Creek Sanitarium in Michigan. Merritt Kellogg himself took training in hydrotherapy, which he used to great success on patients during a smallpox epidemic in 1870. That success inspired him to establish his own hospital. (Courtesy of the Center for Adventist Research.)

First Nursing School Graduates, 1892. The nursing school at St. Helena Hospital began in 1891. At the time, there were fewer than 400 hospital-based nursing education programs in the United States. The first graduating class, pictured here, included (from left to right) Florence Davis-Butz, Lena Tallieur, Amy King, Olif Olsen, Marianna Hermansen-Olsen, and Hazel Spear-Williams. Olif Olsen was the first male nursing graduate in California.

SANITARIUM CALISTHENICS UNIFORM OF 1894. Exercise played an important role in hospital treatments for all maladies. Doctors and nurses alike led patients by example during daily "Swedish movements" routines led by "Miss Bee," the physical activity director labelled here as No 17 at right center. Every worker was encouraged to participate, and uniforms such as the ones modeled here were standard issue.

HOSPITAL STAFF PICNIC, AROUND 1901. Although hospital staff worked very hard, they took time to play. Picnics were a common form of recreation. Because the hospital followed Seventh-day Adventist health principles, meals were vegetarian and generally very light. Sweets were a rare treat but not forbidden. At this picnic, several nurses and a hospital chef display a series of pies that are ready to be served.

GAZEBO AT ST. HELENA SANITARIUM, 1895. John N. Loughborough, an early Adventist pioneer to California, built this gazebo-type garden house and arbor, complete with a central drinking fountain from the Crystal Springs, in 1886. Flowers and seating surrounded the fountain in the center of the building. Loughborough intended the place to serve as a tranquil retreat for patients of the nearby hospital. The gazebo was called Bird House, and it was just one of many outdoor features, which included redwood and oak groves, a terraced rose garden, and a shaded miniature mill pond. Doctors and nurses deemed the outdoor setting so integral to the healing process that oak leaves featured prominently in the hospital logo for many years.

HOSPITAL DINING ROOM, AROUND 1905. A major component of the healing process advocated at St. Helena Hospital was a balanced vegetarian diet. This dining room hosted one particular Thanksgiving Day meal where the menu followed the hospital's health principles. On November 30, 1905, patients and hospital staff celebrated Thanksgiving with a lunchtime meal of stuffed tomato salad, nut bouillon, cream of corn, imitation turkey with dressing, molded rice, and fig preserves.

NURSES IN SWIMSUITS, 1890s. In addition to calisthenics for exercise and health, the doctors, nurses, and patients at St. Helena Hospital took part in plenty of swimming at the hospital pool. This was unsurprising, as one defining feature of Seventh-day Adventist health care was hydrotherapy. This therapy advocated the use of hot and cold water or steam for pain relief and treatment. The curative effects of water applied to both patients and hospital staff, such as the nurses pictured here.

TENTS FOR EARTHQUAKE EVACUEES, 1906. The San Francisco earthquake of April 18, 1906, killed thousands of people and destroyed almost 80 percent of the city. After the initial shocks subsided, fires broke out and burned for days. Refugees and the wounded from San Francisco fled into the North Bay, where they were housed in temporary tent cities. At the St. Helena Hospital, earthquake victims received treatment. Tents such as these served as overflow housing for patients and their families.

SANITARIUM FOOD COMPANY BUILDING AND WORKERS. Diet played an important role in the treatment of St. Helena Hospital patients. Following Seventh-day Adventist ideas about health as proposed by Ellen White, the hospital served only vegetarian food. Since meat substitutes were not widely available at the time, a local food company was established in the 1880s. The company churned out everything from crackers and cereal flakes to peanut-based protein foods like Nuteena. The food factory moved from the hillside to the valley below the hospital in the 1920s, around the time the interior photograph shown below was taken. From left to right, the workers are Will Bogart, Archie Bogart, Oscar Haub, Rob Keller, and Rollins Rose.

ELLEN G. WHITE AT HER ELMSHAVEN WRITING DESK. Ellen G. White, cofounder of the Seventh-day Adventist Church, spent many years on and around Howell Mountain. In 1900, she purchased a home at 125 Glass Mountain Lane from Robert Pratt. She called it Elmshaven after a row of young elms lining the drive, and lived there with her family and many staff members until her death in 1915. In this photograph, White sits at the desk where she penned nine books.

ELMSHAVEN STAFF PICNIC ON THE LAWN. Ellen White did not spend all her time writing. Even in old age, she often traveled by buggy to visit neighbors, accompanied by her assistant of 30 years, Sarah McEnterfer. White's granddaughter later recalled these visits, saying "To needy families she gave lengths of material so they could make clothes for themselves. . . . If they did not know how to sew, she would send some of her office helpers to teach them." White's office staff are pictured here picnicking.

WILLIAM, EDWIN, AND JAMES ANGWIN. Edwin Angwin, pictured here standing over his brothers William (left) and James, immigrated to the United States from Cornwall as a young man. In 1874, he and his wife, Elvira, purchased 200 acres of what he called "the best part" of Rancho La Jota. Here he established a ranch. Impressed by the climate and natural beauty, he built several cabins and a resort hotel to attract Bay Area visitors seeking a rustic getaway.

ANGWIN'S SUMMER RESORT, 1890s. Edwin Angwin built his resort hotel between 1887 and 1889 for a price of $20,000. The finished project could sleep up to 100 guests in comfortable rooms beautifully furnished. The dining room, which seated 150, became popular not only with Angwin's visitors but also with the daily stagecoaches passing over Howell Mountain to Pope Valley. Newspaper ads for the stage promised passengers a stop at Angwin's hotel for lunch.

INSIDE ANGWIN'S SUMMER RESORT, 1900s. Although Angwin's resort promised city-dwellers an escape from everyday life, this did not mean visitors stayed in primitive accommodations. Edwin Angwin decorated his hotel and cabins with fine furniture and elaborate Victorian wallpapers. He even placed a piano in the hotel parlor. In 1895, the St. Helena Star reported that Angwin paid for a telephone line up the mountain "so that his guests may have every convenience afforded elsewhere."

VISITORS AT THE WINDOW TREE. In the fields behind Angwin, this unusual tree beckoned climbers for more than a century. This advertising postcard for Angwin's resort shows guests posing in the usual fashion at the Window Tree around 1900. The tree was so memorable and beloved that the field where it stood is still called Window Tree, even though disease and old age brought it down in 1995.

RESORT STAFF IN 1900. This photograph most likely shows the hotel staff of Angwin's resort around 1900. In the center stands Warren Pope Daugherty and his wife. He wears a white chef's hat, and she has a white and black collar. These are the only staff members whose identities are known.

ENTRANCE TO ANGWIN'S RESORT, 1900S. Angwin's resort proved to be popular. In late August 1887, a *St. Helena Star* article marveled that 25 or 30 guests remained at the hotel, despite the lateness of the season. They attributed this success to the attitude of the proprietors: "Mr. and Mrs. Angwin have the faculty of pleasing and retaining their patrons." Repeat visitors included local district attorney Charles E. Snook and author Ambrose Bierce.

YOUNG PEOPLE AT ANGWIN'S, 1900S. These young people vacationed at Angwin's resort sometime in the early 1900s. Visitors like these were known to be a merry-making bunch. In 1883, the *St. Helena Star* reported that Angwin's guests made the Fourth of July especially festive by stringing flags and Chinese lanterns between their tents, where they glowed "very prettily" at night. Just a few years later, tents were replaced by cabins and Angwin's hotel, where this group stayed.

FRUIT TREES AT EDWIN ANGWIN'S FARM. Edwin Angwin liked to do things himself. An advertisement he ran in the 1889 *San Francisco Examiner* described his newly opened hotel as "constructed entirely from the designs of the proprietor." He was quick to add that it "has already been described by visitors as the most perfect country hotel in California." As for available refreshments, "the table is supplied with milk, fruit, and vegetables from the ranch."

AMONG THE PINES AT ANGWIN'S RESORT. Trails crisscross Howell Mountain, many of them dating to the resort era or the time of the Wappo people. This promotional postcard shows a trail called Pinecrest. A happy resort-goer wearing a straw hat poses in the distance. Edwin Angwin commissioned this postcard as one of a set of hand-colored images advertising recreation spots and beautiful vistas at or near his resort.

HOWELL MOUNTAIN SCHOOL. The Howell Mountain Elementary School was established in 1876 in a little white one-room building near the White Cottages Resort. The children of early pioneering farmers, grape growers, and resort workers attended the school. The roster included the children born to Edwin and Elvira Angwin during their years on Howell Mountain: Rachel, Ethel, Edwin, and Eustace. The building pictured here was replaced in 1957. (Courtesy of the NCHS.)

STAGECOACH IN ANGWIN AND COTTAGE AT AETNA SPRINGS. The stagecoach road over Howell Mountain followed an old Wappo footpath between Napa and Pope Valleys. Later settlers naturally followed the path, widening it for horses and wagons. This was the route followed by the US Army when it marched to and from the Bloody Island Massacre at Clear Lake, where soldiers attacked the Pomo people. In happier times, the road brought vacationers to Howell Mountain and beyond to Pope Valley resorts like world-famous Aetna Springs. The road passed right through the heart of Angwin's resort, where savvy businessman Edwin Angwin made a deal with the stagecoach company. Every traveler, even those bound for Aetna Springs, stopped at Angwin's for lunch in the hotel dining room.

OLD STONE BRIDGE, 1880S. The stone bridge that crosses Conn Creek was built sometime in the 1880s. It featured in postcards advertising Edwin Angwin's resort. The bridge still crosses the creek, but it is now buried under the earth used to make Caiocca Pass. Visitors to Linda Falls from Angwin can view the buried bridge from the hiking path.

FOUR CORNERS OR WINDY GAP. This photograph, taken by George H. Jeys, shows the original, unpaved intersection between Howell Mountain Road and White Cottage Road. The peak in the background is Sentinel Hill, which marked the western boundary of Edwin Angwin's farm. This high point is visible from Napa Valley. Today, Cade Estate Winery is on Sentinel Hill.

Toland House, St. Helena, Cal.

TOLAND HOUSE AT FOUR CORNERS. This postcard shows the Toland House as it appeared in 1904. Located at the junction of what is today Old Howell Mountain Road, White Cottage Road, and Deer Park Road, Toland House served as a rustic destination for Bay Area vacationers at a price of only $6 a week. The proprietors, Thomas McQuie and Millie Toland, were married in Napa in 1884. The resort operated into the 1910s.

In front of Reception Cottage

WHITE COTTAGES
ST. HELENA - CALIF.

THE RECEPTION COTTAGE AT WHITE COTTAGES. White Cottage Road in Angwin is named for the White Cottages Resort near Howell Mountain Elementary School. A 1912 *San Francisco Chronicle* advertisement for the White Cottages boasted an "ideal location," "German cooking," and "automobile excursions" for entertainment. German immigrants J.H. and Margaret Goetsche and Charles Henne were the owners.

WHITE COTTAGES RESORT, 1907. Cofounder J.H. Goetsche opened the White Cottages Resort in 1898. He resided there until his death in 1909, two years after this photograph was taken. Goetsche lived a full life before arriving on Howell Mountain. Born in Germany, he immigrated to the United States in time to serve as a drummer boy in the Civil War. Later adventures led him to invent a nail manufacturing machine, and he also helped lay the first track for San Francisco's cable cars.

HOWELL Mt SPRINGS
THE WHITE COTTAGES

ST. HELENA

SOUTHERN PACIFIC R.R.
NAPA VALLEY ELECTRIC R.R.
SOUTHERN PACIFIC R. R.

NAPA

VALLEJO

BENECIA

MONTICELLO S.S. CO.

PORT COSTA

S. P. R. R.

S. P. R. R.

SAN RAFAEL

SAUSALITO

SAN FRANCISCO

OAKLAND

MAP TO HOWELL MOUNTAIN RESORT, 1900s. Would-be visitors to the many resorts on Howell Mountain faced a long journey to reach their rural destinations. This map from a White Cottages advertisement of the 1910s shows several potential routes that included ferry crossings, train tracks, and winding roads. Most guests would likely catch a surrey ride from the St. Helena train station up the mountain to their vacation spot of choice, but some visitors might have arrived by car. It would not have been a pleasant trip. The first car owner in Angwin brought his 1907 Buick up the mountain hauled by a team of horses because the road was so brutal. One early driver reflected on his trip from St. Helena to Angwin, saying "Three times up the long, dusty road, the longest way up, we stopped to let the engine cool. The dust was ankle deep and concealed the large stones that were underneath. Had to stop to get a breath of clean air if not to let the engine cool."

Log Cottage at Woodworth's, St. Helena, Cal.

LOG COTTAGE AT WOODWORTH'S. Woodworth's resort opened on the Pope Valley side of Howell Mountain around 1900 at the site of the Woodworth and Muller family farm. Like many of the resorts on the mountain, Woodworth's maintained the working farm as both entertainment for guests as well as food for the table. An orchard featuring figs, peaches, apricots, and cherries proved especially popular with the city folks who came to stay.

COTTAGE SCENE AT WOODWORTH'S. Many resort visitors came back annually, drawn by the swimming pool, croquet and tennis courts, outdoor dances, and limitless home cooking. In July 1916, a *St. Helena Star* reporter stayed at Woodworth's and reported on his experience. Meals were served family style, he said, and "[we] just eat and eat, drink milk and cream and rest and every day weigh on the scales that are convenient to the dining room."

50

WOODWORTH'S RUSTIC TENTS. The purpose of a visit to Woodworth's was to immerse oneself in nature, and the resort offered a variety of natural experiences. For the rough-and-tumble visitor, rustic tents with few amenities offered a return to simpler days. However, after power lines were extended from Pacific Union College to the resort, cottage visitors could enjoy electric lights and radio programs while vacationing in the woods.

WOODWORTH'S CROQUET COURT IN WINTER. By the 1930s, mountain resorts waned in popularity due to changing vacation patterns and the Great Depression. After 45 years in operation, the Woodworth and Muller families sold their land to A.L. Dilly. He intended to reopen the resort, but a fire took him by surprise in July 1932. The three-story hotel went up in a blaze before firefighters from Angwin could arrive, spelling the end for Woodworth's.

EDWIN AND ELVIRA ANGWIN AFTER 1909. Edwin and Elvira Angwin chose to close their resort hotel after the summer season of 1909, even though the lucrative heyday of Napa County hotels would continue another 20 years. However, Edwin was nearing 70 years of age. He chose to retire to Berkeley, selling his hotel complete with furnishings, farm equipment, livestock, and parlor piano to the Seventh-day Adventist Church. The resort would be reborn as Pacific Union College.

Four

1909 TO 1949

The 20th century brought with it the closure of many of the resort hotels on Howell Mountain, particularly Angwin's resort. By the summer of 1909, Edwin Angwin was ready for retirement. On August 1, 1909, he sold his acreage and livestock, the resort hotel, and all its outbuildings to the Seventh-day Adventist Church as a new location for Pacific Union College.

The arrival of the college brought a new population to Angwin and with it a building boom. As a result of this influx of students, faculty, and staff, Angwin and its town services saw many improvements. A general store, post office, soda fountain and ice cream parlor, Chevron service station, and more came to Angwin's tiny main street.

Meanwhile, on the hillside overlooking the commercial strip, Pacific Union College expanded its campus from the footprint of the old resort. New buildings constructed from redwood trees felled and milled in the Howell Mountain forests were built by college students working their way through school. These same students hiked through the forest they called "The Thousand Acres," worked for the local businesses, pitched in alongside Napa County locals to fight major fires in 1931, and helped bring in the grape harvest that almost languished on the vine during World War II.

During this era, Prohibition came and went, and the once-dormant wine industry on the mountain began to revive. The St. Helena Hospital expanded, adding more beds and treating more patients. Angwin residents saw their way through the Great Depression as well as two world wars. As the 1950s approached, the postwar shift in American culture began to reach even the slopes of quiet Howell Mountain. For as much as mountain life had already changed, much more excitement lay ahead.

FACULTY AND STUDENTS ON HOTEL STEPS, 1909. Pacific Union College almost did not come to Angwin. When the school board sold the old campus in Healdsburg, Angwin's resort was not yet on the market. During their search for a new location, college leaders considered properties in locations as vastly different as Modesto and San Francisco. They almost purchased the Buena Vista Winery in Sonoma before fortuitously learning about Angwin's property just a month before the new school year commenced.

Angwin's Resort Hotel as Dormitory, 1909. Purchase papers were signed on September 1, 1909, and Pacific Union College opened officially just 28 days later. Transformation from resort to school began immediately. The old hotel became a women's dormitory, while summer cottages housed the men. Faculty taught classes in their living rooms. The faculty also repurposed bowling alley floors into library tables; a bowling ball even found its way to the top of a flagpole.

Pacific Union College in 1912. In the fall of 1909, over 100 acres of Angwin valley farmland was under cultivation. Some early Angwinites reported that the rich soil was 20 feet deep. According to Walter Utt, "five hundred two-quart jars of fruit came with the place and 45 tons of prunes were gathered in the first harvest of the season," to the relief of college president Charles Irwin, who started the school year with a $50 budget.

STUDENTS IN HOTEL DORM ROOM, AROUND 1910. Angwin's resort hotel served as a dormitory for first women and then men until it was demolished and replaced by Grainger Hall in 1923. Ellen White, Adventist church cofounder and PUC supporter, remembered her first sight of the hotel, saying "All the rooms were well planned, and substantially but not extravagantly furnished. Everything about the house and grounds looked clean and wholesome."

FELLING REDWOODS IN THE THOUSAND ACRES. When PUC purchased Angwin's resort, most of the property was covered with forests. There were estimated to be from six to ten million feet of saw-timber, pine, fir, and redwood. Here, from left to right, college woodcutters George B. Taylor, Roscoe Owens, Almon Owens, Harry Smith, and Alonzo Baker pose beside a fallen redwood giant that will be hauled by steam engine to the PUC mill.

PACIFIC UNION COLLEGE SAWMILL, 1910. Although Angwin's resort boasted a small sawmill on the premises, the college almost immediately set about building a larger-capacity mill in 1910. The size and quantity of redwood needed for college construction projects demanded it. Here, from left to right, Walter Peterson, Ignacio Thieleg, Harry Parker, George Wilkinson, and Shun Chin stand in the newly completed Pacific Union College sawmill in 1910.

REDWOOD FRAME FOR GRAF HALL, 1910. Students supervised by Prof. Myron Newton constructed Graf Hall. Almost 20 years later, Alma McKibbin recalled the process, saying "The first big building project was the Girls' Dormitory. . . . Great obstacles were encountered in digging the basement. Boulders and tree roots abounded and yielded only to dynamite. Oh the sweaty, dusty, tired boys I have seen working away in what seemed for a long time only a shapeless hole in the ground."

CAFETERIA IN GRAF HALL, 1920S. Since 1895, the Pacific Union College cafeteria has only served vegetarian meals to its students. This typical dinner from the dining hall menu board around 1920 was no exception. Students could look forward to a meal of vegetable oyster soup, cranberry beans, mashed potatoes and gravy, beets, Spanish rice, apple and nut salad, cream of chocolate pie (one order per person strictly enforced), and prune whip. Prune whip is an old-fashioned classic that combined puréed prunes with sugar, egg whites, cream of tartar, and a squeeze of lemon. As for the vegetarian oyster soup, that mysterious recipe is lost to time.

College Press in 1918. The first printing press came to Angwin around 1917 as a gift from Ellen White to her twin grandsons Herbert and Henry. They brought the press to college with them and left it as a gift upon graduation. In this photograph, the Whites and several classmates work on the first edition of the *Mountain Echo*, a school newspaper and yearbook hybrid that was published until the 1930s. The college press was also responsible for printing the *Pacific Union Recorder*, the official organ of the Seventh-day Adventist Church in California and other parts of the West. The *Recorder* was published in Angwin until the closure of the press in the 1980s.

LLOYD MARTIN HARVESTS HAY, 1910. The college dairy provided its cattle with alfalfa hay grown on over 50 acres of farmland, including the fields across from campus. A typical harvest, such as the one of June 1932, often exceeded 250 tons of hay. The harvest pictured here was the first ever at PUC. Lloyd Martin, a student in 1909–1910, earned about 15¢ an hour mowing hay for the college dairy cattle.

TRACTOR STUCK IN THE MUD, 1927. The winter of 1927 saw constant heavy rainfall, which turned Angwin's earth into thick, yellow mud. In February, the college farm debated buying a second team of horses to help pull the plough. Instead, it purchased this used Fordson tractor for $200. "It is in good shape, the new paint is still on," the *Campus Chronicle* reported. However, even the old Fordson was apparently no match for the mud.

STUDENTS TEND BEAN VINES, 1920. Planted by Edwin Angwin to feed visitors to his resort, this prune orchard and farm passed to Pacific Union College in 1909. Students worked on the farm not only to provide food for the college cafeteria but also to earn tuition funds for their schooling. In the late 19th and early 20th century, it was common for vines to be trellised on redwood stakes. Pamphlets from the era often advertised four-foot-long stakes for sale at $20 for 1,000. These stakes, however, were cut for free by Edwin Angwin in the local forest. The stakes served the college well, as redwood could be reused for many years. In fact, almost a century later, when David Abreu purchased land from the college and set about establishing his Las Posadas Howell Mountain vineyard, he uncovered a long-lost stockpile of old-growth redwood stakes from these early days. Perhaps he found the very stakes pictured here.

Angwin's Main Street, 1920s. This view shows Angwin's main thoroughfare. In this photograph taken from the stairs to Irwin Hall, cars are parked outside Old West Hall. This building housed the general store and post office until it was inundated by a mudslide in the 1930s. Today, the road still runs through the center of Pacific Union College's campus. West Hall Annex now stands on Old West Hall's foundation.

COLLEGE SERVICE STATION, 1920S. The old barn from Angwin's resort enjoyed many rebirths over the years. Originally home to Angwin's dairy cattle, it continued to serve Pacific Union College's herd for a while. Then it was reimagined and reused as a photography studio, temporary student housing, and finally the college garage and service station. It was demolished in 1940, and Chan Shun Hall now stands in its location.

WORLD WAR I VETERANS ON ARMISTICE DAY, 1919. The end of World War I bore great significance for Angwin, as many college students had paused their studies in order to fight. On November 11, 1918, the college celebrated the Armistice by ringing the school bell while students marched down Angwin's main street singing patriotic songs. On the anniversary in 1919, Professor Newton decorated each ex-serviceman present with a green and gold ribbon. They were photographed in uniform as seen here.

St. Helena Sanitarium in 1918. When the Rural Health Retreat first opened its doors in 1878, the simple two-story wood-frame structure served only a dozen patients at a time. With the expansion of services and coinciding construction projects, the hospital grew. In this photograph, the original health retreat building with its tower is visible on the far left, and additions are on the right. The original building continued to be used until 1968.

First Sanitarium Automobile, 1913. The journey up Howell Mountain to reach the St. Helena Sanitarium could be steep and grueling. To help everyone arrive safely and in comfort, the "San" sent transportation into the valley to meet guests at the St. Helena train depot. In 1913, the usual horse and buggy was replaced for the first time with an automobile, pictured here. Howell Mountain roads were not paved until the 1930s, so the open-air auto certainly took guests for a dusty and exciting ride.

GRADUATING NURSES IN 1914. This graduating class of 1914 was the first to receive diplomas from the newly accredited St. Helena Sanitarium and Hospital Training School for Nurses. Although the school opened its doors in 1891, accreditation with the state became standard much later. On September 15, 1914, the hospital nursing school celebrated its official status, and at that time, a school pin was adopted.

CRYSTAL SPRINGS NURSES' HOME, 1918. This postcard shows the building that housed hospital staff and students of the nursing school. In the waning days of World War I, a nursing student named Lottie mailed this postcard to a soldier friend who was fighting in France. She wrote "This is our 'New Home,' looking at you from the hillside. . . . It's some fine building. . . . Room for all the girls and all full too. Be sure to come and see us when you come back from France."

NURSES DURING SPANISH FLU, 1918. Victims of the 1918 influenza pandemic, sometimes called the "Spanish flu," received treatment at the St. Helena Hospital. Doctors there prescribed strict bed rest, a regulated vegetarian diet, and hot and cold hydrotherapy treatments provided by a nurse who monitored patients' care. Meanwhile, the *Weekly Calistogan* advocated "onions, lots of them. We have them every day, raw, chopped fine, plain or with vinegar." They ended with a piece of worrisome advice: "Don't be afraid to eat them."

SANITARIUM BAND ON JULY 4, 1917 OR 1918. For many years, the community of Sanitarium relished its tradition of a Fourth of July concert and program hosted by the hospital. In this photograph from the 1917 or 1918 Fourth of July, the Sanitarium band warms up and gets into formation in front of the San Laundry building. These annual programs continued for at least 40 years.

DAILY EXERCISES FOR SANITARIUM STAFF. John Harvey Kellogg of the Battle Creek Sanitarium invented more than corn flakes. He also advocated a regimen of outdoor calisthenics that would offset daily caloric intake. Although the St. Helena Sanitarium was founded by a different Kellogg brother, its staff adopted a similar system of fresh air exercise. Patients were encouraged to join in, with a set of "passive exercises" modified for those too feeble to stand.

VIEW OF GLASS MOUNTAIN FROM SANITARIUM. This view, captured from the balconies of the St. Helena Sanitarium, shows several local landmarks. On the right, Elmshaven is recognizable with its three-story tower. The upper room of that tower served as Ellen White's writing room. On the far left is the Sanitarium Food Company factory. The hill rising in the foreground is Glass Mountain, a popular destination among nursing school students for hikes and hayrides.

ELLEN WHITE AND FAMILY, AUGUST 24, 1913. This photograph of Adventist Church cofounder Ellen White and her family was taken at her Elmshaven home in 1913. From left to right are (first row) Virgil Robinson, Francis White, Arthur White, and Grace White; (second row) Dores Robinson, Ella Mae White Robinson, Ellen White, May Lacey White, and Willie C. White; (third row) Mable Workman, Wilfred Workman, Henry White, and Herbert White.

SANITARIUM ELEMENTARY SCHOOL, 1920s. In response to requests from St. Helena Hospital workers, a small Adventist elementary school opened in 1901 in the community of Sanitarium. Ten grades were taught in small classes that often averaged fewer than a dozen students. A *Pacific Union Recorder* article from April 1910 cheerfully reported, "The Sanitarium school will undoubtedly turn out the largest eighth grade graduating class in the conference this year. If we are rightly informed there are fifteen or sixteen." Today, this school is Foothills Elementary.

PACIFIC UNION COLLEGE ELEMENTARY SCHOOL, 1916. This photograph shows elementary students gathered at the Angwin's hotel entrance. At this time, the elementary school met in the old resort dance hall, right in the heart of campus. Before occupying the dance hall, the "grammar grades" met in Nevada Cottage. The room was so cramped that Anna Newton taught while standing in a doorway. It took until 1927 for a dedicated elementary school to be built.

LAS POSADAS FOREST 4H CAMP, 1929. When Mrs. Anson Blake donated Las Posadas Forest to the State of California, it boasted a thick second-growth forest. In her gift, Blake stipulated that the forest be used for research rather than recreation, with only one exception. A 4H camp was to be established to serve Bay Area counties. This 1929 photograph shows one of the first summer programs held in the camp, which remains active today. (Courtesy of the Jack Mason Museum of West Marin History.)

SACK RACE, 1914, AND NOAH AND MARY PAULIN, 1935. Picnics were a popular Angwin pastime. During the early years at Pacific Union College, one never knew when the president might cancel classes for the day and declare an impromptu picnic. Other times, the students and staff gathered for special-occasion picnics to celebrate holidays or graduating seniors. These events always drew a crowd, which often included most of Angwin, since so many residents were connected with the college. Festivities such as foot races came before big potluck dinners that were served from blankets spread in the grass. In the photograph above, young people compete in a sack race. Below, impeccably dressed music professor Noah Paulin shares a cup of tea with his wife, Mary.

HOSPITAL PHARMACY WORKERS PLAY IN SNOW, 1930s. Although a large hospital formed the center of the tiny town of Sanitarium, it was indeed a community where people lived as well as worked. This photograph shows hospital pharmacy employees Mr. and Mrs. Edwards playing outside their home after a particularly heavy snowfall in the 1930s. Hospital brochures from the 1930s and 1940s describe the Edwards' hometown as "a considerable village occupied by the [hospital] itself and its many retainers. So skillfully hidden are these buildings scattered and hidden among the trees of the mountainside that the effect is distinctly that of restful rusticity—and natural beauty." Even so, Sanitarium boasted a "general store, garages, laundry, post office, and powerhouse, as well as the homes of employees" like these pharmacy workers.

W.I. Smith Plays Baseball, 1930s. This photograph of Pacific Union College president W.I. Smith playing baseball is a bit of a miracle. In early years, the college forbade anyone to play competitive games on campus. Pres. Charles Irwin in the 1915 yearbook recorded that "the discarding of games, and the substitution of useful labor therefore, has had a beneficial effect" on the student body. Luckily this sentiment had passed by the 1930s.

PUC Preparatory School Graduates, 1935. These high school graduates were the first to leave the new Pacific Union College Preparatory Academy. Previously, PUC Prep existed solely as a part of the college, but in 1934, it became independent and began to thrive under Principal Lloyd Downs. A few years later, the current high school building was constructed and named McKibbin Hall after Angwin pioneer Alma McKibbin.

STUDENTS VISIT OVERHANGING ROCK AND BUZZARD'S ROOST. A brisk walk through Howell Mountain forests proved a favorite pastime for young and old alike, particularly if the walk provided a view. An issue of the *Pacific Union Recorder* in 1918 advertised the delights of local destinations such as Overhanging Rock (left) and Buzzard's Roost (below), saying, "In the loveliest season of the year, one may stroll through the woods on a Sabbath afternoon to one of the many places of interest and beauty surrounding the College. The most noted of these perhaps is the Falls, which is about one half hour's walk from the campus. A short distance from here is Overhanging Rock, where a view of almost the entire Napa Valley may be obtained. Or one may go in the opposite direction to Buzzard's Rest, and view in panorama Pope Valley, with its ranges of mountains beyond."

WOODCUTTERS AND FIREWOOD, 1920s. For many years, a boiler provided heat to the Pacific Union College campus. Student lumberjacks cut wood to feed the boiler all winter long. However, in 1931, a wildfire burned up the east side of Howell Mountain and consumed 900 cords of wood prepared to stock the boiler that winter. After this disaster, the college switched to a much safer oil burner, and the incidence of axe wounds decreased.

ANGWIN FIRE DEPARTMENT, 1948. The big fire of 1931 also prompted the creation of Angwin's first official volunteer fire department. The college and surrounding communities from Angwin to Sanitarium joined together to raise funds. They raised over $1,000 toward stationing a state fire truck in the area. This volunteer force, which later combined with the college campus fire brigade, was the predecessor of today's Angwin Volunteer Fire Department.

ROAD TO ST. HELENA ON A FOGGY MORNING. Discerning wine connoisseurs can taste the differences between valley floor and mountain-grown grapes. Valley grapes are bright and ripe, with a heavy feel on the palate. Mountain grapes are darker, with more acidity and tannins. This is because marine-layer fog, as pictured here, from the San Francisco Bay often covers only the valley and lower slopes. This means that nights on Howell Mountain's peak are often warm and clear.

FRIESEN LAKES, 1945. Dick Friesen purchased the White Cottages resort and surrounding land from C.A. Henne in 1933. Noticing the many creeks crisscrossing his land, he set up dams to create lakes. By the 1940s, he ran a private water company that distributed water to Pacific Union College and local addresses. In 1985, the Angwin community purchased Friesen's private company, forming the Howell Mountain Mutual Water Company.

SANITARIUM ROAD, 1943. Located between Angwin and St. Helena on the slopes of Howell Mountain, the community of Sanitarium thrived in the shadow of St. Helena Sanitarium. Formerly named Crystal Springs, the village was renamed and granted the post office designation of Sanitarium from 1901 to 1970. It is now known as Deer Park, although the road that runs past the hospital still bears the old Sanitarium name.

ANGWIN AND PACIFIC UNION COLLEGE, AROUND 1935. Before the construction of Angwin's airstrip in the 1960s, enterprising folks who wanted to photograph the whole college and town had to hike up the hills ringing Angwin's "crater." This photograph may have been taken near today's Viola Way. The view shows farmland and the college before the county road moved to its current location. Many buildings in the background still stand today, but the foreground has changed significantly since 1935.

WORLD'S FAIR LAMP IN ANGWIN, 1940s. The streetlamps seen in these photographs came from the Golden Gate International Exposition, held on Treasure Island from 1939 to 1940. When the festivities closed, Pacific Union College purchased these lamps with their distinctive textured glass globes. Biology professor Ervil Clark made metal shades that could be affixed to the lanterns like the petals of a Diogenes' lantern, as seen at left, in honor of the school flower. For many years, the college celebrated Homecoming Weekend with these embellishments. The photograph below, which features three students playing in the snow, shows a standard World's Fair lamp without flower petals. Thanks to the restoration efforts of the college facilities staff, many of these original 1939 lights remain on the campus today.

RED DELICIOUS

BICKFORD RANCH

HOWELL MOUNTAIN

BICKFORD RANCH APPLE CRATE LABEL, 1940S. The Bickford ranchers of Ink Grade Road were among the many locals who earned a statewide reputation for excellent fruit. A *Weekly Calistogan* article from 1922 reported that A.G. Haskell's orchard, behind the White Cottages resort, sent nine varieties of apple to the county fair and won nine blue ribbons. By 1932, twenty-three varieties of Howell Mountain apples formed the centerpiece of the California State Fair fruit display.

MEDICAL CADET CORPS REVIEW BY WEST HALL, 1942. With the outbreak of World War II, Pacific Union College established a Medical Cadet Corps program. The Medical Cadet Corps was invented in the 1930s by Everett Dick, a Seventh-day Adventist from Nebraska who wanted to prepare pacifists to become medics if they were drafted into the armed services. At Pacific Union College, retired Navy captain C. Roscoe Hyatt and college physician Dr. Mary McReynolds started

the Angwin branch of the program. In addition to medical training, the cadets received daily drills, as seen here in May 1942. The training proved necessary. By September 1942, seventy-five college students had been drafted. By the end of the war, that number would reach more than four hundred.

STUDENTS STUDY OUTSIDE GRAF HALL, 1943. On the home front, everyone supported the war effort. An empty patch of ground next to the college service station was transformed into a Victory Garden cultivated by faculty members. The manager of Angwin's general store, I.C. Immerson, led a series of successful war bond drives. Meanwhile, young women like these supported their friends on the front lines by observing nightly blackouts and hiding in the woods during air raid practice.

MEDICAL CADET CORPS, 1940s. In regions where there was enough interest, the Medical Cadet Corps expanded its ranks to train women as well as men. The women of PUC's Medical Cadet Corps took the same courses as the men, but they marched, drilled, and trained in skirts. Some of their training exercises were complex. In 1942, the town of St. Helena staged a practice evacuation. "Victims" were treated onsite by cadets before transfer to St. Helena Hospital.

Five

1950 TO 1989

As the country emerged from World War II, a new era of American prosperity kicked into motion. Even quiet Howell Mountain would see changes from top to bottom, some of them surprising. The town of Angwin began to expand as the G.I. Bill brought waves of returning veterans to Pacific Union College. Enrollment eventually peaked in the 1970s with over 2,200 students packing into dormitories like sardines. With an increase of students came more jobs at the college, spurring the creation of neighborhoods like Hillcrest and Sky Oaks.

The newly arrived Angwinites brought innovation, which they turned toward bettering their town. They established the Angwin Chamber of Commerce and opened a local chapter of the Kiwanis Club. Some joined the Angwin Flyers Club, which successfully convinced the college to build an airstrip in March 1961. Meanwhile, farther down the mountain, the community of Sanitarium watched as the historic health retreat from 1878 was removed and replaced by a brand-new hospital building worthy of a new name. The town followed suit in 1970, becoming Deer Park.

With a commercial and population boom across Napa County came concerns about the natural environment. These concerns coalesced into Ordinance 274, resulting in the Napa Agricultural Preserve, established in 1968. The Angwin Chamber of Commerce was the first chamber to support the ordinance. A few years later, in 1976, longtime Angwin resident Duane Cronk joined other like-minded environmentalists to establish the Land Trust of Napa County.

These early movements presaged concerns that would soon come to a head on Howell Mountain. But for now, locals simply celebrated the moment in 1984 when the Howell Mountain American Viticultural Area (AVA) became the first sub-appellation with the Napa Valley AVA. With fine wine, a new hospital, and a bustling college, life on the mountain gleamed golden as the century drew to a close.

ANGWIN AND PACIFIC UNION COLLEGE, JULY 1969. In this view of Angwin, the new college church (right) dominates the landscape with its stark design by architect Alfred Johnson. A program from the church opening states, "the simplicity of the structure with minimal stained glass and a complete lack of costly architectural frills made it possible to build economically. At the same time the worshiper feels a sense of reverence as he enters the sanctuary with its gothic feel." The bunker-like building certainly contrasted sharply with the architectural style of other buildings in the heart of Angwin. The college underwent major redesigns throughout the 1930s to 1950s resulting in the flat-roofed stucco look across most of the campus, a true blend of art deco and mid-century styles.

NEW CHEVRON STATION, 1952. Angwin's main gas and service station moved into fresh quarters in the fall of 1952. After decades of cramped and congested conditions in its old location, the opening of a new stretch of Howell Mountain Road made expansion and modernization possible. In addition to taking the Chevron name, the new station boasted two gas pumps, blacktop driveways and parking, and a service station with a lift. The *Campus Chronicle* reported that "both the inside and outside of the station have recently been painted yellow trimmed in green," and "the office and servicing departments have large plate glass windows to permit ample natural light."

HOWELL MOUNTAIN ROAD OPENS, 1949. On October 13, 1949, an estimated crowd of 200 Angwinites turned out to cheer the first cars to drive a new stretch of Howell Mountain Road. The bypass began at the old 1880s stone bridge over Conn Creek and cut through the fields west of the college, avoiding the congestion of the original road that passed through the busy heart of campus. Celebrations began with songs played by the college band. Speeches followed, featuring county engineer E.P. Ball and Angwin Chamber of Commerce president H.W. Clark, among others. The speakers thanked Charles Tamagni, Angwin's member on the Napa County Board of Supervisors, for his untiring efforts in raising funds for the road. At precisely 1:49 p.m., Tamagni cut the ribbon, and the road opened to traffic. Cars driven by county, community, and college officials and students made an informal parade through town.

Placing Three Water Tube Boilers, 1950. The building boom that came to Angwin after World War II extended as far as the college heating plant, which was purchased as a complete unit from Hammer Field in Fresno. Engineer W.H. Cordis carried out the transportation project. Students, faculty, and staff pitched in to help dismantle and reassemble everything, including an eight-foot-tall steel stack.

Pacific Auditorium, 1951. Pacific Union College benefited greatly from the disposal of surplus government property after World War II. The new gymnasium pictured here was one such thrifty purchase, although Pres. Percy Christian had a hard time convincing the college board to purchase the oddly shaped building from Camp Parks, where it had served as part of a blimp hangar. The college reassembled the gymnasium on the site of the old baseball diamond. It opened i

PACIFIC UNION COLLEGE DAIRY, 1950. The College Dairy brand served Howell Mountain communities fresh dairy products for most of the 20th century. The first dairy cattle came with Pacific Union College's purchase from Edwin Angwin, and the barn was in the center of campus until it was destroyed by arson in 1949. The new milking building pictured here opened in 1950, and marked the official move of the college farm from the heart of Angwin to the fields near Veteran Heights and Mill Valley.

ENTRANCE TO VETERAN HEIGHTS, 1940s. After World War II, the G.I. Bill brought a surge of enrollment to Pacific Union College and a population boom to Angwin. Since many of the returning veterans were older students, they often brought spouses and children. To make affordable housing for these families, Pacific Union College built the neighborhood of Veteran Heights and filled it with Quonset Huts–turned–homes. Residents became self-sufficient. They elected their own mayor, built a chapel, and opened a commissary.

HOME ECONOMICS COOKING CLASS, 1960. The home economics major at Pacific Union College was established in 1944. Although classes were offered on the topic prior to World War II, the large number of women attending college in the postwar years made it popular. The college soon added degrees in secretarial science and library science to appeal to women entering the workforce.

PACIFIC UNION COLLEGE ELEMENTARY SCHOOL, 1958. This photograph shows the PUC Elementary School multigrade classroom during the era of Principal Alice Neilsen. For many years, education majors from neighboring Pacific Union College came to the multigrade room to complete their student teaching and perform observations. In a way, this blended classroom was a "lab for prospective teachers," as recalled by Alice Neilsen's niece Cheryl Daley.

PREPARATORY ACADEMY CHRISTMAS PAGEANT. Elementary, high school, and college events provided a steady stream of entertainment for Angwin residents. Most were open to the public, creating a connection between school and community. These family-friendly events included the annual Hawaiian Program, the Adventure film lecture series, the Artist Concert Series, which featured well-known classical musicians, and many talent shows, Christmas programs, school picnics, and more.

SODA FOUNTAIN IN NEW SHOPPING CENTER, 1960. The proprietors of Angwin's soda fountains received a steady stream of customers from Pacific Union College. The shop pictured here opened in 1956, but the first fountain of note operated in the 1930s. It was so popular that an irritated local wrote to college president W.E. Nelson demanding that he stop the students from "sucking down ice cream" between classes. Nelson replied that he enjoyed the occasional milkshake himself.

HILLTOP CENTER AT 400 COLLEGE AVENUE, 1955. A curious white building stands on the corner of College Avenue and Clark Way. It is the former Hilltop Center, which operated throughout the 1950s. It opened across from the furniture factory on Circle Drive, which is now the Village Church. The Hilltop Center supplied factory workers and neighborhood folks with groceries and gas, and attracted college students to its soda fountain.

College Mercantile Hardware Store, 1950s. Angwin's local hardware store has been a part of the Ace Hardware Cooperative since 1980, but its beginnings go back much further. The College Mercantile always boasted a hardware section sufficient to keep locals supplied for modest home repairs and construction projects. When the shopping center on the corner of College Avenue and Howell Mountain Road opened in 1956, the hardware store got its first dedicated storefront at last.

PLANTING DAWN REDWOODS AT PUC AND SANITARIUM, 1954. The Angwin Founders Day celebrations of April 1954 included a ceremonial planting of five dawn redwoods on the Pacific Union College campus. The seedlings were gifted by alumnus Donly Gray of Gray Nurseries in Elverta, California. Gray received the seeds from Dr. Ralph Chaney of the University of California, who collected them in China. Chaney attended the planting at PUC and gave a speech explaining how the dawn redwood was previously thought extinct until its rediscovery in China under Chiang Kai-Shek in 1944. Gray, pictured here with hat in hand, was born in 1879 to Harvey and Emma Hurd Gray, who were instrumental in establishing St. Helena Hospital and the Pacific Press. To honor their memories, he donated these seedlings to PUC along with several more to St. Helena Hospital in 1954.

NEW HOSPITAL WING, BUILT 1969. In 1969, this 90-year-old hospital received a major upgrade with the construction of a new wing. The addition housed the St. Helena Center for Health, now called the St. Helena Lifestyle Medicine Institute. Its purpose was to emphasize personal and community wellness. The same year, the hospital shed the name "Sanitarium," which it had since 1898, becoming St. Helena Hospital. A domino-like effect brought about further changes, as the community lost its distinctive Sanitarium post office designation in 1970. It is now known as Deer Park, although addresses read St. Helena. Now, only the road passing the hospital still bears the Sanitarium name as an homage to almost a century of history.

Nurse Gives Daily Health Lecture, 1939. To aid in full-body healing and lifelong health, hospital staff hosted a series of weeknight lectures on topics ranging from proper posture to breathing techniques. Here, a nurse speaks to an audience of patients and staff on the dangers of eating between meals and the benefits of fruits and vegetables.

Nursing Uniforms from 1891 to 1940s. The St. Helena Hospital nursing school celebrated its 50th anniversary in the 1940s, so students and staff modeled uniforms from the past. From left to right are (first row, in uniforms from 1905 and the 1890s) Joyce Dillon, Sue Neuman, Bert Miller, Lucille Phariss, and Martha Johnson; (second row, in treatment room dress and uniforms from 1907 to 1925) Beth Joiner, Dorothy Sneed, Hilda Pittendrigh, Ruth Cockran, Eva Woesner, Ms. Wallin, Rhoda Craig, and Blossom Glass; (third row, in uniforms of the 1940s) Irene Robson, Naomi Gowan, Victor Duerksen, Lucile Lewis, Kiyoko Nishikawa, and Gertrude Wallin.

REENACTORS AT HOSPITAL DIAMOND JUBILEE, 1953. The St. Helena Hospital, then called the Rural Health Retreat, opened its doors on June 7, 1878, on a shelf on a 10-acre tract of mountain land at Crystal Springs donated by William A. Pratt. According to one account, there were already 14 prospective patients waiting at the St. Helena train station on opening day. The hospital sent a team of horses and a three-seated spring wagon to the station to carry the guests up the two-and-a-half-mile road to the retreat for the very first time. Seventy-five years later, during the hospital's diamond jubilee in 1953, William A. Pratt's surviving children dressed in period clothing and gathered in a similar wagon for a celebratory photograph. Pratt descendants present that day, from left to right, were Homer Pratt of Calistoga (seated), Clara Rose, Amy Meyers, and Ron Kilgore. They are pictured with a hospital administrator in a contemporary suit.

ELMSHAVEN, NATIONAL HISTORIC LANDMARK. After Ellen White's death in 1915, her home was maintained by the Ellen G. White Estate, a governing body in charge of publishing and managing White's many books and manuscripts. The estate remained at Elmshaven until 1938, after which time the home gained popularity as a tourist destination. White's granddaughter Grace White Jacques served as tour guide. Elmshaven hosted educational groups such as the student reenactors pictured here. In 1993, the home was declared a national historic landmark.

AERIAL VIEW OF GROWING ANGWIN, 1957. This May 1957 aerial view of Angwin, taken by R.L. Reynolds, showcases the town's most recent construction projects. At far left is the new shopping center with soda fountain, beauty parlor, and post office. On the right, the running track is beginning to take shape. Later, the Angwin Flying Club used this photograph to successfully propose an airstrip on the hill above campus.

AERONAUTICS SUMMER WORKSHOP, 1968. Angwin's airstrip officially opened in 1961, making it possible for Pacific Union College to offer a degree in aviation. Dr. Richard Fisher, second from right, ran the program through the Industrial Arts Department. This photograph was taken in August 1968 during a summer workshop where pilots from Travis Air Force Base and Lockheed Corporation offered specialized training.

MISSION PLANE DEDICATION, 1963. The first Seventh-day Adventist mission plane sent to South America was dedicated at the Angwin airstrip in 1963. It was named after Fernando Stahl, the first Adventist missionary to Peru. In 1966, James Aitken published a book about this plane titled *White Wings, Green Jungle.*

AIRPORT PANCAKE BREAKFAST, 1962. On July 15, 1962, the Angwin Flyers Club hosted a fly-in and air show at the Angwin airport, Virgil O. Parrett Field. Forty pilots and their planes participated in the event, which included skydiving, stunt flying, and a display of antique aircraft. The Angwin Chamber of Commerce supported the Flyers Club by hosting a pancake breakfast in the brand-new hangar. This photograph of the breakfast was taken by L.R. Callender.

HERSCHEL HUGHES AND THE THINKER, 1961. In 1961, Herschel Hughes was a graduating senior as well as president of the Men of Grainger, the men's club at Pacific Union College. As a parting gift to his alma mater, he created this "twentieth-century interpretation of Rodin" that he called *The Modern Thinker*. The statue instantly gained cult-like status on campus. It became popular to paint and repaint the statue as a rite of passage.

DEDICATION OF NEW POST OFFICE, 1969. Angwin's current post office building officially opened for business on July 2, 1969. Congressman Phillip Burton cut the ribbon and gave a speech. He shared the stage with representatives from other Angwin entities such as Frakes Aviation, the new Bank of America branch, and the chamber of commerce. Postmaster Ray Balch accepted a new 50-star flag from Congressman Burton, and a Pathfinder color guard raised the flag while Pacific Union College choral director Carolyn Bisel sang the national anthem. In the weeks before the event, the *St. Helena Star* published articles advertising the occasion, which helped to draw a sizable crowd for the dedication and festivities. These photographs were published later in a commemorative booklet.

New Angwin Shopping Center, 1970s. Angwin's commercial center moved into new quarters in 1976 with the completion of the new Angwin Plaza. This prime spot on Howell Mountain Road placed the College Mercantile, the Bank of America branch, and the laundromat in the center of town at last. When Bank of America moved out less than a decade later, the locally owned Silverado Credit Union (established in 1953) took over this location, where it remains to this day.

College Mercantile, 1979. The move to new quarters caused a boom in business for the College Mercantile. Throughout the early 1970s, sales increased by about 20 percent per year, according to manager Lester Birney. However, rising fuel costs later in the decade caused weekend sales to bottom out. Apparently, out-of-towners hesitated to make the trip, even though this was the only completely vegetarian market in the county.

CELEBRATING AMERICA'S BICENTENNIAL, 1976. As part of Angwin's celebration of the bicentennial, the Pacific Union College institutional public relations class purchased this Bennington flag and presented it to the school. The flag featured 13 red and white stripes and 11 stars. This was the first stars-and-stripes flag used in battle by land forces during the Revolutionary War. Here, students from the class present the flag during an assembly. They are joined by their professor, Herb Ford, on the right.

RADIO STATION KANG REPORTS ELECTION, 1978. The election of November 1978 carried special weight for Howell Mountain residents, as a local name appeared on the ballot. Dr. Norma Bork, a professor in the communication department, ran for US Congress. Radio station KANG reported results from its Angwin studios. Bork lost to incumbent Donald Clausen with 45 percent of the vote.

CAMPAIGN PHOTOGRAPHS FOR NORMA BORK, 1978. Dr. Norma Bork ran for Congress again in 1980. She competed with Donald Clausen once again as well. The race was challenging, especially considering that the Second Congressional District is so large. At the time, the district encompassed six counties, and covered territory from San Francisco Bay up through most of Northern California. While Dr. Bork enjoyed name recognition on Howell Mountain and throughout Napa County, her Republican opponent was defending a seat he had already won three times before. On election night 1980, Norma Bork took home 10,000 more votes than she had in 1978, but to no avail. Clausen won the election. Perhaps surprisingly, Clausen also won in Angwin. The town's election results showed a clear preference for the Republican candidate, as he handily defeated local candidate Dr. Bork by 600 votes.

GIRLS ON CORNER OF ANGWIN AVENUE, 1973. The corner of Angwin Avenue has always posed a challenge to commuters. Prior to 1980, campus visitors entered through this guard gate, showing an ID card for access. However, the gate and island were removed in 1980 because, according to the *Campus Chronicle*, cars making lefthand turns from Howell Mountain Road tended to "cut out the corner too short and straddle the island," getting very inconveniently hung up.

CAMPUS MALL AND FOUNTAIN FROM IRWIN HALL. When the county road moved to its current location, visitors suddenly approached PUC from behind. In response, Pres. F.O. Rittenhouse spearheaded the construction of the mall, complete with lighted fountain. The project took over three years to complete. The fountain was the final touch. Installed on November 6, 1969, the fountain fell victim to a practical joke only hours later, when some unnamed student filled it with soap. Repairs cost $10,000.

CLUB OFFICERS POSE BY FOUNTAIN, 1974. In 1970, Pacific Union College students formed the Afro-American Club. Rolando Henry served as the first president. He described the club's purpose, saying "We, the Black students of Pacific Union College, as Christians and as Black Americans, see the need for gathering our forces so as to intoxicate mankind with that brotherly love which makes all men equal." Pictured here are the club officers of 1974. Today, the club continues as the Black Student Union.

ANGWIN TO ANGWISH RACE, 1970s. The Angwin to Angwish trail run began in 1974 as a joint effort organized by the members of Collegiate Adventists for Better Living and the Napa Running Club. The first year's route followed eight miles of paved streets, fire roads, and dirt trails through Howell Mountain forests. The route included the steep and challenging Angwish Hill. The race occurred annually through the 1980s, fell out of favor for a time, and returned in the 2010s.

DISCOVERYLAND PRESCHOOL, 1980S. Angwin's Discoveryland preschool was established in 1973 as a learning lab for early childhood education majors at Pacific Union College. The preschool enjoyed so much popularity that by 1990 it employed seven staff members and cared for 35 students. That same year, under the guidance of director Shelley Reynolds, the preschool became fully licensed by the state. Discoveryland still operates at its Cold Springs Road location.

KEN KENNEDY IN THE SNOW, 1982. Howell Mountain winters used to see more snowfall. The student newspaper, *Campus Chronicle*, eagerly reported every dusting of flakes, and Pacific Union College students always took full advantage of opportunities for snowball fights on campus. Here, student Ken Kennedy frolics in the snow in front of Newton Hall in February 1982.

Milton McHenry and Lorraine Mitchell, 1977. When the baby boomers reached college age, Pacific Union College reached peak enrollment numbers, swelling the population of Angwin considerably. When the college opened its doors in September 1909, only 42 students were present. By 1975, more than 2,200 young people were enrolled. In this photograph, financial counselor Milton McHenry prepares incoming student Lorraine Mitchell for the new school year.

Family in Veteran Heights, 1970s. The neighborhood of Veteran Heights, renamed Mobile Manor, was meant to be temporary housing. However, Angwin's postwar population boom never receded. In addition to the Veteran Heights neighborhood, Liparita, Sky Oaks, Sunset, and Willeta subdivisions were all expanded. Mobile homes replaced Quonset huts at Veteran Heights, and a small, close-knit community continues to live there today.

PUC Elementary School Parade, 1978. In a small town like Angwin, the entire community turns out for school events, even those hosted by the private Seventh-day Adventist elementary school. This parade in 1979 is one example. The college newspaper reported a large turnout for the day of festivities, which included a craft show, dog obedience trials, and a food fair in addition to the parade down Howell Mountain Road.

COLLEGE CENTENNIAL CELEBRATIONS, 1982. Pacific Union College first opened its doors in April 1882 at its original location in Healdsburg, California. In April 1982, the college celebrated its centennial anniversary during Homecoming Weekend. Over 3,000 alumni planned to attend the festivities, which included a vintage car parade, displays of college memorabilia, and a speech by historian and author Walter Utt.

DEMOLITION OF IRWIN HALL, 1982.
Sadly, Pacific Union College's centennial year saw the demolition of the front half of Irwin Hall. From its construction in the 1910s, this building served the college as church and chapel, administrative offices, classrooms, library, and so much more. In fact, Irwin Hall's facade featured prominently in the college logo throughout most of the mid-century. During the summer of 1982, it was partially demolished as a result of dry rot and significant sinkage. Alumni and locals were devastated.

STUDENT AND COLLEGE CHURCH, 1986. The Pacific Union College Adventist Church sits at the heart of campus, easily seen from the county road. Before its construction began in 1965, Angwin Adventists had no dedicated church building. Although the church sanctuary doors opened in 1969, the overall project took almost 20 years to complete. At the time of this photograph, the Reiger organ was newly installed and work was finally considered done.

ANGWIN TOWN SIGN, 1970s. This well-known local landmark was installed in the 1970s at the corner of Cold Springs and Howell Mountain Roads where visitors enter Angwin's main street. Many Angwin residents collaborated to make the sign a reality. Duane Cronk provided the initial design, which the Angwin Community Council okayed. Wally Specht laid the stone, and Art Goulard planned the plantings and lighting. Artist Clyde Provonsha rendered the design, adding the flower on a whim. The flower is the *Calochortus amabilis* or Diogenes' lantern, the Pacific Union College school flower since 1923. This rare plant grows prolifically on Howell Mountain.

Student Milks Cow at College Dairy, 1970s. In 1986, after 77 years in operation, the Pacific Union College Dairy closed its doors. The closure came as part of a government buyout spurred by excess milk impacting the market. Angwinites mourned the loss of plentiful local milk, and college students looked back in nostalgia. One former student employee of the dairy, Jon Scully, was disappointed. "It was fun working with the cows," he said.

Six

1990 to 2020

When the Pacific Union College Dairy closed in 1986, it seemed to indicate a drift away from connection to the land. The departure of the last cow marked the end of a dairy that had operated since Edwin Angwin's days. At the same time, college students were increasingly likely to pursue a career in nursing, medicine, or the emerging tech field rather than agriculture. Pacific Union College began to consider selling land.

Down the hill at St. Helena Hospital, an increasing number of trespassing hikers threatened the water supply. This led to the closure of the popular hiking trail to Devil's Punchbowl, which entered the hospital's private property. Changing cultural expectations about private property also closed access to Overhanging Rock. To some observers, it seemed that Howell Mountain's natural environment was shrinking on all sides.

However, behind closed doors, lovers of the land began to act. Local grape growers sensed the importance of advocating for and protecting their mountain. They banded together in 2004 to create the Howell Mountain Vintners and Growers Association under a mission statement that included increased "awareness and interest in the Howell Mountain AVA's unique terroir." When Save Rural Angwin (SRA) formed just three years later, its mission focused on promoting the unique character of the town's "central open space, agricultural focus, and wooded setting." The group's lobbying efforts resulted in the passage of measures that would protect Angwin for years.

At last, inspired by an outpouring of alumni sentiment as well as the actions of SRA, Pacific Union College reconsidered selling its forested land. In a complete reversal of position, PUC instead joined forces with the Land Trust of Napa Valley and CalFire to create a conservation easement that preserved nearly 1,000 acres of unbroken wilderness, woods, and hiking trails. Shortly thereafter, Howell Mountain Farms launched its Angwin farm stand in the old college creamery building. The doors to the dairy were open once again.

STUDENTS ON IRWIN HALL STEPS, 1990s. For 30 years, Pacific Union College letterhead and promotional material were emblazoned with an image of Irwin Hall. However, after the building facade was demolished, it was time to refresh. The college entered the 1990s with a new logo featuring a tree within a gothic arch. The tree image symbolized a shift in focus from buildings back to the forests and fields of the college's Howell Mountain home.

RASMUSSEN ART GALLERY SHOW, 2000. Since it was built in 1974, the Rasmussen Art Gallery on the Pacific Union College campus has housed exhibits for established artists as well as students. Many artists have called Angwin home over the years, and their work is often featured at the gallery. One wing is named for Vernon Nye, a prize-winning California watercolorist who helped establish the college art department.

MOVING THE COLLEGE PRESIDENT'S HOUSE, 1968. In November 2005, the old Pacific Union College president's house burned down. The home, called Wawona Cottage, was built in 1914 at the base of the Irwin Hall stairs in the heart of campus. Six college presidents lived in that house over a period spanning 44 years. In 1968, the house was moved from the college to the corner of Newton and Bay Streets.

ANGWIN VOLUNTEER FIRE DEPARTMENT. Howell Mountain is served by two robust volunteer fire departments. One is in Deer Park near St. Helena Hospital. The other serves the town of Angwin and surrounding areas. During the severe California wildfires of the last decade, Howell Mountain firefighters were among those on the front lines in Napa County and beyond. In the late summer of 2020, the LNU Complex Fire threatened to sweep past Aetna Springs and over the mountain, prompting a mass evacuation of all Howell Mountain residents for the first time in living memory. During that traumatic time, the volunteer firefighters of Angwin and Deer Park stayed behind and watched their communities despite the danger.

SHOPPING CENTER SIGN BEFORE AND AFTER REDESIGN. Angwin's shopping center underwent several moves, rebuilds, and redesigns throughout the years. The latest came in the summer of 2017, when the college officially changed the name of the store to the Howell Mountain Market and Deli. College chief financial officer Brandon Parker explained the change, saying "With the opening of the Deli, we felt the time was right to consider updating the name. Our surrounding community has grown significantly in recent years, and so has our Market. We felt the time had come to change the name to more accurately reflect that fact that we serve the needs of a much larger community than just the college." During the coronavirus pandemic of 2020, the reach of Angwin's market became apparent. When many Napa Valley grocery stores struggled to stock eggs and toilet paper, locals from miles around trekked to Angwin, where the Howell Mountain Market often still offered essentials.

SAVE THE WINDOW TREE. The Window Tree, which entertained generations of Angwin's resort guests, locals, and college students, began to fail in the 1980s. In an effort to save the iconic tree, the college put up a fence and a sign begging visitors not to climb into the branches. In July 1995, the tree succumbed to old age, fungus, and rot. It was removed, although the meadow where it once grew is still called Window Tree on college maps. PUC Preparatory Academy continued to call its yearbook *Window Tree* until 2016.

STUDENTS AT INSPIRATION POINT, 2010s. New safety requirements led to the installation of a guardrail around Inspiration Point in recent years. Meanwhile, small madrones and scrub oaks grew up from the cliff face and blocked the scenic outlook. The view was improved and reopened by PUC professor of emergency services Matthew Russell and student Alex Nelson in March 2020. Inspiration Point once again provides valley views from a safe vantage point.

BIKERS, 1990s. In the 1990s, mountain bikers discovered the forests and trails of Howell Mountain. Locals long knew about such hidden gems as the Whoop De Doos, Heartbreak Hill, Gobo's Revenge, and Angwish, but the maze of trails was poorly marked and unmapped for years. Rico Mundy's 1994 map of the Back 40 popularized the trails with mountain bikers and began to draw visitors from the valley and beyond. Further improvements in recent years have included new, clear signage on the trails and an official map published by Pacific Union College. The trails remain open to the public and serve as a welcome destination for locals and Napa Valley tourists.

ANGWIN ADVOCATE DUANE CRONK. Any conversation about the rural quietude of Angwin must mention Duane Cronk. A resident of Howell Mountain since 1962, Cronk became a local legend. For decades, he deployed his background and skills in public relations on behalf of nature and the preservation of agricultural land. He was a founding member of the Land Trust of Napa County, Upper Napa Valley Associates, and the public action committee Save Rural Angwin, which campaigns on behalf of the natural environment by limiting development. Cronk also loved storytelling and photography. He channeled these passions into his website, the Angwin Reporter, which served the community as an irreplaceable goldmine of local news. He also published the *Angwin Telephone Book* from 1993 to 2015. When Duane Cronk died in 2018, the mountain lost a kindhearted advocate, an endless font of jokes and stories, a friend, and a neighbor.

HOWELL MOUNTAIN FARMS, 2020. Under the capable direction of Doug Helmer, seen above watering seedlings, Howell Mountain Farms takes shape at its new home on the hill above Angwin. The farm relocated in 2019 from its former location near Helmer and Sons Construction. Now plants flourish in the fields near the old PUC creamery, which is being remodeled into a farm stand for the local community. A greenhouse is planned as well as a propagation house. Produce from Howell Mountain Farms already serves local restaurants such as Auberge du Soleil, and fresh vegetables can also be purchased at the Howell Mountain Market and Deli in the heart of Angwin.

NATIVE PLANT GARDEN, 2018. Aimee Wyrick Brownsworth, a biology professor at Pacific Union College, spearheaded the replanting of a garden space outside the Angwin Post Office. Beginning in 2018, she collaborated with college students and local gardeners to remove invasive or foreign species from the garden, replacing each plant with native California varieties.

PUC FOREST TRAIL DEDICATION, 2019. A crowd gathered in October 2019 to celebrate the dedication of a new trail through the Pacific Union College forest. This three-mile addition linked two sections of the Bay Area Ridge Trail, an extensive hiking route from Calistoga in the north all the way to Gilroy in the south.

HIKING THE CONSERVATION EASEMENT TRAILS, 2019. In 2018, Pacific Union College collaborated with the Land Trust of Napa County and CalFire to finalize a conservation easement agreement that protects almost 1,000 acres of its forests in perpetuity. With the conservation easement come a series of other improvements, including a shaded fire break that will protect mountain residents from wildfires that might otherwise threaten their homes.

Selected Bibliography

Conaway, James. *Napa*. Boston, MA: Houghton Mifflin, 1990.

Dillon, Richard H. *Napa Valley's Natives*. Fairfield, CA: James Stevenson Publisher, 2001.

Driver, Harold E. *Wappo Ethnography*. Berkeley, CA: University of California Press, 1936.

Haynes, Irene. *Ghost Wineries of Napa Valley: A Photographic Tour of the 19th Century*. San Francisco, CA: S. Taylor & Friends, 1980.

Heizer, Robert, ed. *The Archaeology of the Napa Region*. Berkeley, CA: University of California Press, 1953.

Kunkel, Fred, and J.E. Upson. *Geology and Ground Water in Napa and Sonoma Valleys, Napa and Sonoma Counties, California*. Washington, DC: United States Geological Survey, 1960.

Patillo, Chris. "Elmshaven (HALS CA-94)." Historic American Landscapes Survey, National Park Service, US Department of the Interior, 2013.

St. Helena Hospital. *St. Helena Hospital Celebrates 130 Years of Remarkable Medicine*. Deer Park, CA: St. Helena Hospital, 2008.

Utt, Walter. *A Mountain, a Pickax, a College*. Nampa, ID: Pacific Press Publishing Association, 1996.

Weber, Lin. *Old Napa Valley: the History to 1900*. St. Helena, CA: Wine Ventures Publishing, 1998.

Wright, Elizabeth Cyrus. *Early Upper Napa Valley: A Sketch from the Archives of the Napa County Historical Society*. Napa, CA: Napa County Historical Society, 1979.

Discover Thousands of Local History Books
Featuring Millions of Vintage Images

Arcadia Publishing, the leading local history publisher in the United States, is committed to making history accessible and meaningful through publishing books that celebrate and preserve the heritage of America's people and places.

Find more books like this at
www.arcadiapublishing.com

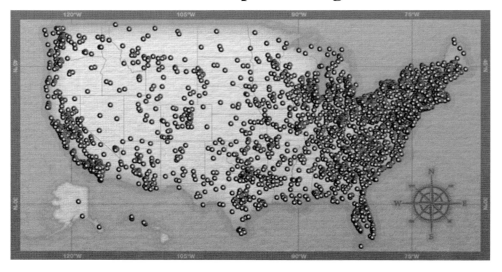

Search for your hometown history, your old stomping grounds, and even your favorite sports team.